Missing Moments

Missing Moment: Poetry in the Key of Me

Copyright © 2016 Allen Smuckler

Photos by Allen Smuckler

Book and Cover Design by Nick DeSimone

ISBN-13: 978-0578188423

ISBN-10: 0578188422

Smuckaduck, Inc.

Missing Moments
Poetry in the Key of Me

Allen Smuckler

SMUCKADUCK, INC.

SARASOTA, FL

"sometimes i don't know, which moment
which cool gust of wind will come,
and enchant me
tousling my hair
and my heart,

stirring...that familiar ache of poetry,

which drop will kiss
the old wrench in my soul
reminding me, all over again

i miss you better in the rain."

- Sanober Khan

*This book is dedicated to
my family and friends,
without whom, I would be a solitary soul.*

Contents

Preface

Missing Moments: Poetry in the Key of Me set out to be a book of not only missing and unfinished poems, but also a missing part of my life, the child-rearing years… Unfortunately, working two and three jobs, helping to raise three children, and the general upkeep of a home, writing took a backseat and only occasionally did I write a poem. This, in hindsight, was something I would regret, for I missed the most important aspect of my life, recording in words, my children growing up and capturing their daily experiences and silly, profound and noteworthy events that took place between the years 1975 and 1997. Thank goodness for camcorders and my 35 mm Canon camera, otherwise I would only have my fading memory to remember those important moments. To say that was a mistake would be an understatement, but quite frankly I thought my writing days were behind me. I also missed 35 years of teaching moments which, in their way, were as humorous, heartwarming, and emotional as family.

I also changed the look of the title to Missing MOMents, implying the book was in memory of my mother who lived with Alzheimer's for nine years before her passing in 2006. When editing this book, I came to the realization that only one poem was written about, to or in memory of my mother, *Fragments of Light*, so I changed the title to remove the caps. I just thought it would be unfair and disingenuous to my mother and her memory.

So then, what is *Missing Moments* about and how did it come to be *In the Key of Me*? It is a collection of poems divided into six chapters; Time, Life, Loss, Despair, Hope and Love. Each chapter is ordered by date (earliest to latest) to tell about different parts of life as seen through my ever evolving eyes, from the emotional, idealistic, impetuous, teenage years to my cynical, cautious, leisurely years of retirement. Like my first book *Unknown Journey: A Voyage Through Time*, each chapter shows my growth and development of not only form and style but my changes in emotion, pain, loss, hope and love. My early poems are just that, raw, sophomoric, aching while my more recent are more refined, thoughtful, and healing.
I hope they touch your heart, heal a wound or make you smile.

Foreword

Socrates stated that, "The unexamined life is not worth living." In this latest book of poetry, Allen Smuckler demonstrates for us his investment in living the reflective life. The arrangement of the book allows him to share these examinations over wide expanses of time and through diverse lenses. By including the un-retouched works produced at various periods in his life, Smuckler invites us to assess the maturation of his craft and his humanity. We see in these works the struggle of someone trying to give voice to feelings of desire and despair, love and loss, faith and hope. That voice is at times a whisper and at others, a shout, sometimes repeating words or phrases when a single iteration isn't sufficient. Many poems in this volume lend themselves to easy interpretation but others require unpacking and re-reading. We are also likely to find our own emotions captured in various pieces and may sometimes wince at what we discover.

The photographs that accompany several of the pieces allow for additional reflection. In his segments on Time and Life, Smuckler's poems seem to provide a sometimes whimsical, sometimes aloof commentary on life and experiences. The segments on Loss and Despair turn darker and at the same time, more personal. Amid his struggles, Smuckler's words sometimes reach out in faith to address unanswerable questions. In the next section on Hope, he, like many of us, seems to be imploring himself to believe rather than trying to express an affirmation. The final segment on Love is refreshingly broad. Rather than limiting the topic to the romantic love between soul mates (which he does address), Smuckler casts a wider net to encompass the love of a parent, of a child, of a family, and of the capacity for giving love itself. It's an appropriate culmination for this reflection on life and one that seems far from over.

Chuck Miceli
President, Osher Lifelong Learning Institute at UConn
Editorial Board chairman – Voices and Visions
Author, *Amanda's Room*
June, 2016

Introduction
Missing Moments: Poetry in the Key of Me.

(Viewpoints on this work of Allen Smuckler)

This book of poems divides up well into six parts. To a degree the reader finds a poetic growth from adolescent to adult, although I find it difficult not to admire some facet of each poem. What I do note about myself as a reader is that I want to read the next poem, I want to continue in the world of imagination and reality that the poet offers in a frank and often powerful way. As with almost any poet, there are phrases and images that stand out, and comments about life that strike the reader's conscience. This latter moment is when I find myself smiling at the words in front of me. These are the moments that Allen Smuckler molds images of his life into a memorable figure; these are the moments for which I recommend this work. At times I think the poet lives too much in the mundane clichés of everyday life — and yet that is what makes the collection valid, for the poems do not shy away from telling truths about life.

Rhyme, alliteration and other literary techniques are to be found amid Smuckler's lines, yet it is their usage that proves the poet a wiser man than most, a keener observer of relationships that bind him to his personal world. From the chuckles I yield when reading "Remote", yes the television remote, to the undeniable revelations of "Fences", the poet's honesty must strike the reader with a wish to re-read a poem; the urge to continue reading Missing Moments does not fade. Even the brutal thoughts within "Squirrel" intrigue rather than repulse me; even the simplicity of some of the early poems elicit the truths from youthfulness. This volume holds its own among the loose abstractions of the latest poetic publications.

B. Lindsay Denyer
Poet, artist, teacher
April 2016

Brian passed away shortly after he wrote this introduction for me. He had become a mentor, a confidante, and a fellow poet who was always there to offer feedback, suggestions and support. Most of all however, Brian was a friend and he will be dearly missed.

TIME

Sometimes you will never know the value of a moment until it becomes a memory.

- Theodor Seuss Geisel
Dr. Seuss
American writer and illustrator
(March 2, 1904 – September 24, 1991)

Ringling Museum
Sarasota, Florida

Perplexity #2

sitting under a decaying tree

looking and gazing at my surroundings
I see and hear only the silence of the forest

I often wonder and ponder what succeeds life
and realize that man and certainly I
were not created to conquer such perplexities.

God placed man in His image upon His creation to
attain and absorb the knowledge and complexities
but in His infinite wisdom forgot to acquaint us with
certain mysteries

often difficult to comprehend, I seek awareness which
would master my soul, educate my mind
and heal my heart …

one perplexing thought permeates
and frightens

life is just a fleeting
moment

compared to death's everlasting
presence …

January 13, 1968 — 18 years old

Time
(a haiku)

Fill your life with love
scale the ultimate beauty –
in time find peace

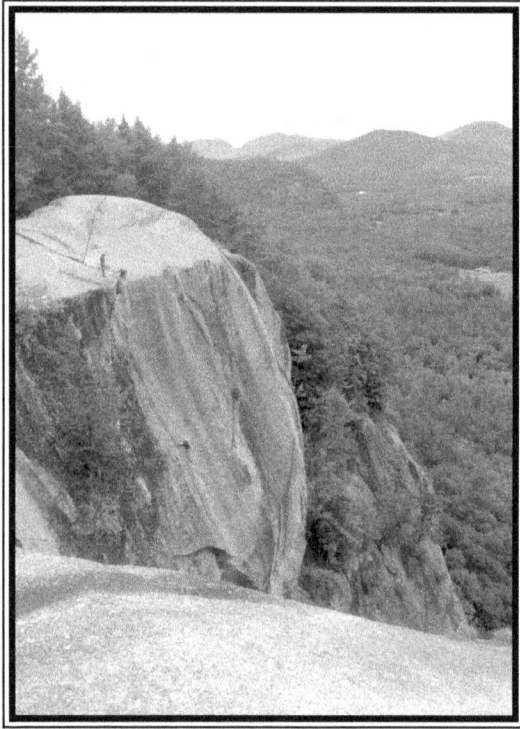

***Echo Lake State Park and White Mountains
Conway New Hampshire***

November 10, 1969

Secreted Thoughts

Tempered nights
clashing against
peace-ridden skies,
Ancient, endless shades
echoing in those
meager times
we once knew
and once loved,
a long time ago.

Silk covered days
on the streets
and cow pastures
of life's distractions-
stopping on the way
for a cup of tea
at a sidewalk café
that we once shared,
a long time ago.

Broken nights
on the edge of
our drifting past.
Collages of lights
on every corner
telling us it's all a play
and we as actors,

remember when
we were young,

such a long time ago.

April 8, 1972

time...endless time

a
    ru (ss) ian
                        class (stud) on-l-y (ies) to   (le
)arn   ss(ru)ian   .

the wat ch keeps time;
                            n
                          d
                          l
                            e
                              s
                                s   t.......i..........m..........e...............

b   u   t   4   w
                                                        h
                                                        a
                                                        t ???????

se (sun) ize   the   gnizalb

                            &
put (i) t   to
                                rest;

en (moon) gulf   the   (face (less)

                            &
sac) fice (ri   4or   the

                    s   p   s.
                                                                    t
        ,s   t   &   l   e
                                                                    a   n

                r   a
WAIT a   (min)
                        I
                          'vе   (ute)!   NeVeR
tak (en   u
        a   class
                                                                s
                                                            ian

February 15, 1974

Allen Smuckler

Sunset
Siesta Key, Florida

Lost in Time

Somewhere
(between)

night
&
day

June of '03
and December '08

appears
a gap in time
that leaves me
forgetting
why
I'm
here
&
where I've
been…

Do you remember?

January 24, 2010

Allen Smuckler

Fool

At that taxidermal pool,
awaited words; looked the fool.
Found a chaise, faced the sun,
boiled skin, a touch of drool.

Bonita Springs, acting cool,
away from cold, snow, and Yule.
Basked and baked; finally done,
aloof children cutting school.

Ten more minutes, as a rule,
owl stood guard on his stool.
It used to be so much fun,
I am camped without my fuel.

Brayed and stubborn like a mule,
drenched as if under wool.
Had to leave; better run,
first I better wake up, fool!

January 12, 2011

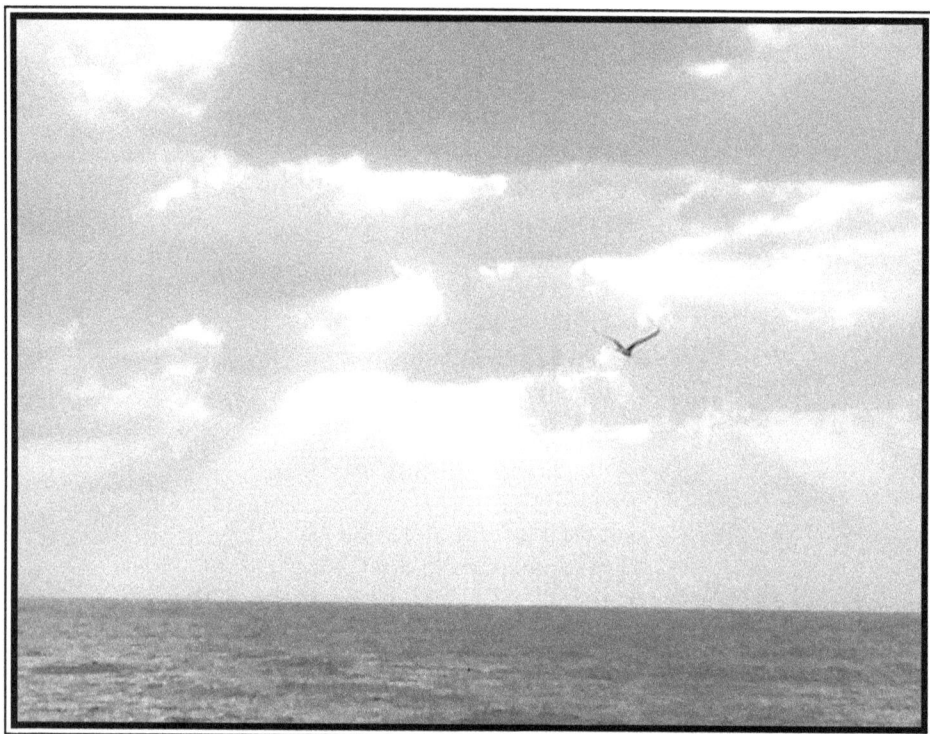

Turtle Beach
Sarasota, Florida

Allen Smuckler

It's never too late

The warmth of the day
scorches Siesta Key Beach

waves splash upon the shore,
winter melts into spring

... somewhere

and I ...

I continue to

soar
with the gulls,

swim
with the dolphins,

fish
with the wrens,

&

aim (less) ly

drift
amongst
the clouds -

realizing at last

It's never too late

January 13, 2013

remote

we're not going to
find
what it's like to be
kind.

when it's time to
unwind

it's there for the making

if you have the
mind.

life's enchanted
as our bodies
combine

mystified

as our lives
intertwine

pass the remote, please

signs ... stated
deeds ... dated
nothing left to do

Heart ... sated
time ... wasted
only thoughts of you

pass the remote ...
if you dare

July 10, 2013

Allen Smuckler

Away

Away, away
away we flow
through time and space
all else we know
eternally
we go away…

Hello. Hello?
Is it really you
that touched my heart
throughout the years?
Lovingly
you went away.

Goodbye, take flight,
it felt so right.
I'm not ashamed
to seize the day.
Eventually
I ran away

Away, away
away we split,
rejoiced the time
we had with each,
not mourn the days
we stayed away

Away, I never
thought I'd live
away or get to see
that extra day.
I praise the Lord
for that…and more

and wish I weren't
so far away…

August 29, 2013

13

Siesta Key
Sarasota, Florida

Allen Smuckler

Waves of Endearment

EMPHATIC w   v   s
                a   e
emblematically
collidingwith the stoicshore
of Siesta Key Beach…
Melodic, enabling waves
coughing and hacking
heavily upon the shore.
        c
    r   h
A   ing their bodacious
brassy bodies,
cresting & **climaxing**
to levels of
complacency and disrespect.
a
n
gling toward the
established order of time…
long forgotten, e r o d e d
by the
Waning wAvEs
washed wistfully
away by the passing
of time,
unable to recall
or recognize
f
    a
        lling lines ___ ___ ___
And death … always playing its part
settles and seethes in the dust b   l
                                  o w
of humanity and normalcy.
The lines begin their endless quest
rising from the nadir to the crest.
The clouds o < pen, skies brighten
and the avenue of angels sing.
Unnamed, unknown, unseen
the angels sing.

March 26, 2014

Oy Vey

Oy Vey, what a day
splishing and splashing
against the walls of time.
The more I work, I sigh
understanding at last -
I should laugh
instead of cry.

My body's aching,
my patience waning,
time passing slowly
watching eggshell paint dry.

Oy Vey, as I begin flaying.
Prepping and painting
when I should be playing.
All I can do
is hope and pray
that the colors
are here to stay.

Oh boy, it's such a joy;
the two-toned room complete.
It's better than I thought -
with one final realization;
this passing pleasure
was exceeded only
by the
tortuous tedium.

July 9, 2015

LIFE

In the end, it's not the years in your life that count. It's the life in your years.

- Abraham Lincoln
16th President of the United States
(2/12/1809 – assassinated 4/15/1865)

Tanka 1

Eagles overhead
viewing tides and morning dew -
I am the sunrise
children play beneath my rays
rainbows shade the golden pond.

Alaska

April 3, 1979

Allen Smuckler

Disappointment Turned to Joy

Sliding and slithering,
the windy road glided
quiescently beneath
the snail-like car.
The destination:
a stony cliff
covered by copious,
cumulus clouds.
The purpose: pursue
the summer sun
on its routine journey
beyond the rolling hills.
    Once I reach the
      r   d
     a   e
      g g   cliffs
of West Rock Park, which overlooked
the sleeping hamlet of New Haven.
The sky ominously deepened and
clouds continued to blanket the earth.

Suddenly, a rumble.
the 1st drop splashed
   serendipitously
to moisten my nose.
The 2nd licked my ear,
while the 3rd & 4th
tickled my tongue.
A sprinkle ensued.
Counting became comical.

An incessant shower
rinsed away
the day's useless toil,
thunder clapped its approval.

…Moments passed, when I
rose to my feet, shuffled aimlessly
to my Pontiac Tempest …
and rolled
for the ride home,
a diminutive number.

June 5, 1972

19

Red Crested Mama

Red Crested mama
pecked at
her suet,
saved and served
her children the
morsels.
Tended her young
set the
table for three,
labored as if
she'd do it
forever.
Stifled and lifeless
listless and faded …
the
red crested mama
pecked at
the suet…

She succeeded
at will
but not life
as we
knew it.

June 5, 2013

Allen Smuckler

Squirrel

Hey squirrel!
Diggly, wiggly squirrel,
gray as my mood,
get out of my yard,
my neighborhood,
my life…
You're not welcomed
here for
countless reasons.
Doesn't matter
the range of seasons.
You scrounge for nuts,
dig up my grass,
let's face it squirrel,
you're a pain
in my ass.
You bother the
birds' feeders
and their space,
destroy the lawn
to bury your stash

Perhaps Mr. Squirrel
you'd prefer in its place
a '22 pointed
at your cute little face.

October 5, 2013

Tanka 2

Reflection
in a crystalline mirror;
sculpted mountain
entreats upon the current
on its breathless perfect way

Ketchikan, Alaska

June 17, 2014

Allen Smuckler

Marauding Menaces of Summer

The multiple stings of the
yellow jacket with its
empty and humorless
unimportant examination of
the queen's venomous,
pollinated menagerie.

Meaningless inside my
motionless membrane,
smarting but not impossible,
biting rather than stinging,
for his … or her
diabolical pleasure and
contemptible demands.
Its mosaic, impolite mind
miffed at morning's mist,
mesmerized by its own
humiliating moroseness.

I mindfully muse, that
Home Depot markets an
ingenious though not quite
humane gimmick manufactured with
allurements meant to murder
these tormentors of summer.
"hmmmm," I murmured,
and merrily mapped my destination.

"May I have multifarious amounts
with multitudes of replacements?",
I charmingly asked the merchant.
"Most definitely," as he muttered:
"may your mass-murdering of
these metastasized malignancies
make you mirthful and mellow."

I smiled ☺

and meandered home in a
meaningful and methodical manner.
Setting the mythical traps of mayhem,
the vermin began to pile motionlessly
in mounds of their own enigmatic
imagery.
I smiled again in a manner
reminiscent of
a maniac, as I whistled a melody
of contentment and amusement.

August 10, 2014

Flirting with Life

Part of the
decorative distinction
between recognizing
the bewildering emphasis
stuck on the rock ledge
of discovery, and
finding the eternal glow
which reaches the
recess of our minds …
is that person
who believes all is
well with the world;
no complaining,
no arguing,
no compromising
between right and wrong,

just pulverizing
the juxtaposition
of what remains.
Finding how to
approach the salient
philosophies, blending
estuaries of time.

Vanishing from creative
yet mundane structures
of misinformation,
we try our best
not to entangle what
we cannot understand, while
forging through the wintery,
woeful, weather of wistfulness.

July 1, 2015

Allen Smuckler

Butchart Gardens
Victoria, British Columbia

Another Birthday

Birthdays, seem to come and go
Love is always here to stay
Birthday seas ebb and flow
Love, in fact, decides the way

Birthdays try to tell no lies
Love, we say, belongs to us
Birthdays steadfast on the rise
Love, and joy, without the fuss

Birthdays proudly show the gray
Love, like elk, is colorblind
Birthdays teach me what to say
Love, abounds, and so divine

Birthday wishes on my lips
Love reminds me to forgive
Birthdays from your body drip
Love is all I want to give

September 10, 2015

LOSS

It is so much darker when a light goes out than it would have been if it had never shone.

- John Steinbeck
The Winter of our Discontent
American author
(2/27/1902 – 12/20/1968)

Fences

Softly you're spinning your web
miscues, deception and fright.
Your heart relating a tale,
my eyes completing the sale.

I'm frightened, I must admit,
losing what I think must be right.
Where are we going from here?
Why are we feeling such fear?

Tenderly, needing to part,
flickering out of the light
Deciding to figure it out,
wondering what it's about.

Staying together for years,
trying with all of our might.
Escaping what must be me.
Everything always a we.

Dreaming or living a lie,
always appearing so bright.
Washing my being away,
causing my body to stray.

Finally, facing the world,
travelling into the night.
Thinking of me all alone,
wasting the time I don't own.

Parting in sorrow, and love,
leaving at last from your sight.
Aiming to reach for my star,
feigning we aren't what we are.

April 23, 2011

Allen Smuckler

...to

...to
his emptiness
and shallow promises
hoping at long last
he has finally grown
from
the boy his father knew
...to
the man he never was...

Along
the way
he left a path of
destruction and pain
lies and deceit
perpetual motion
...to
stagnation and resignation

...to
pretend to be
a writer in the storm
rescuing those
in his path only
...to
destroy those
that
he loved and
left behind...

October 1, 2013

Au Revoir

Adoring love and precious kisses,
planning long and peaceful nights …

Drifting stages, thoughtful gazes,
making love, transcending time …

Reaping thoughts within my mind,
classic image on another stage …

Plasticene panes and mighty rushes,
from a tapestried life of childproof days …

Au revoir my dear, good-bye for now …
Au revoir my love,

Au revoir …

May 8, 2013

Allen Smuckler

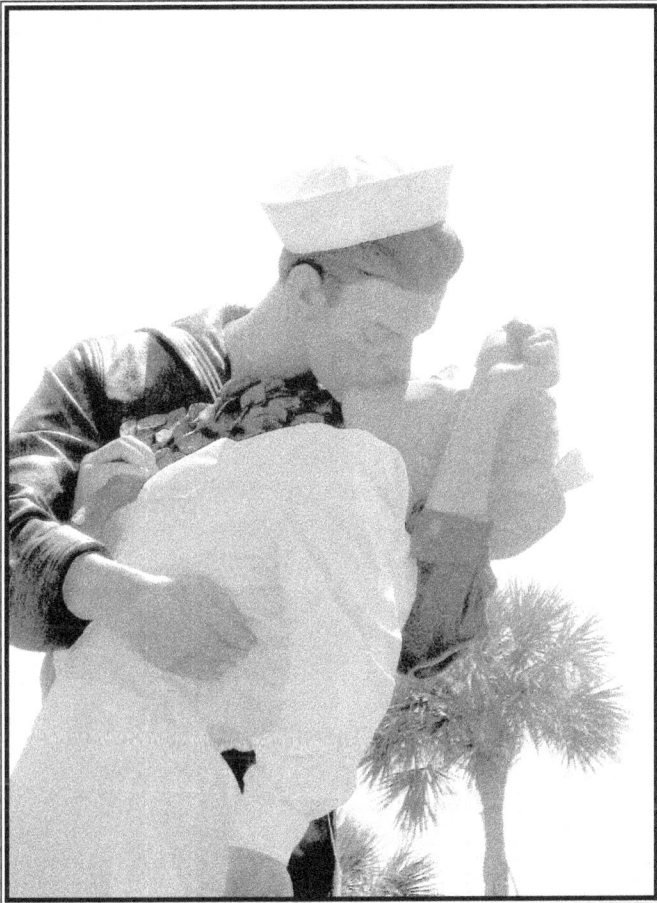

Sarasota, Florida

Amongst The Ruins

You'll never really know
why I sit amongst the ruins
and cry. The answers never
realized. The pampered tunes
never die. While I
bequeath myself
amongst the ruins
and play those harmful games.

It's never going
to be the same
amongst the ruins of my
dismay and shame. Whatever's
done can't be undone
nor shared with anyone. It seems
to be just make believe
amongst the ruins of our lives.

As that fateful day is hung to
dry on the branch of seamless
rhyme. I sit alone amongst the
ruins to figure out our time.
Until we meet again,
in this life or beyond,
to sleep and dream
amongst the ruins
as clouds romance the sky,

I'll think of you and miss
the days … that started long ago.

October 6, 2013

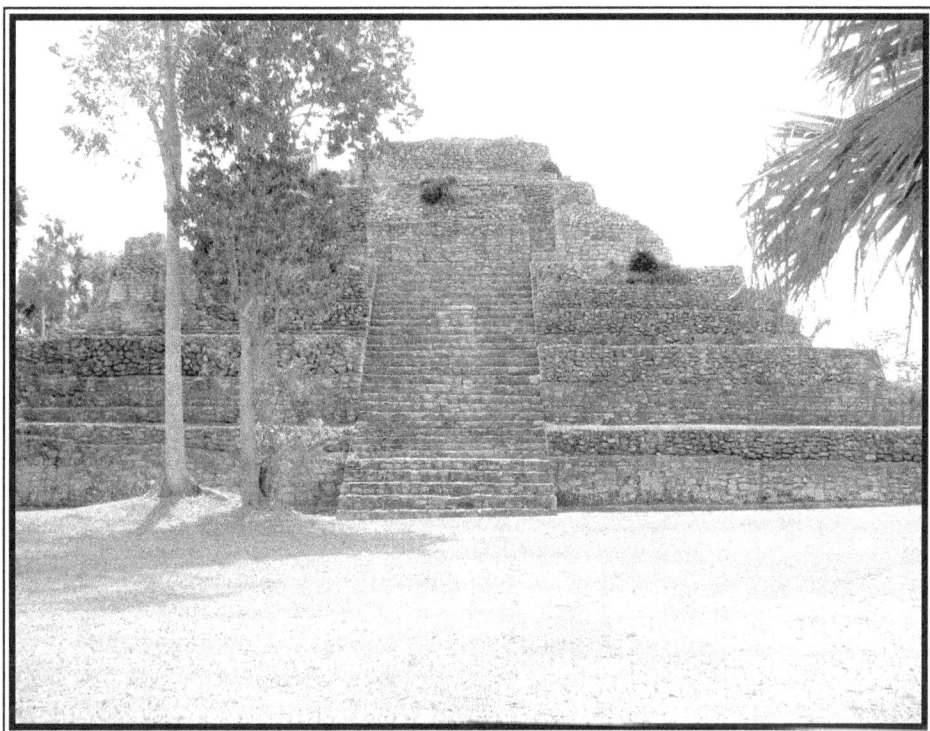

Costa Maya, Mexico

Missing Moments (too)

I've missed the time
we spent together;
the love, the hugs
the invitations.
Sitting on logs, benches,
on the beach, while
the boats unleash
from their piers
of attachment.
I spend those
missing moments
questioning aloud
the how and why
I became so lost
in this dream,
and let you go
disappearing through time
never tasting the nectar,
walking the puppy,
viewing the morn;
benevolent beliefs
we were not alone
when we were.
Understanding those
shared missing moments.
Knowing from the start
they would cease to be
nothing more than missing moments;
and exist no more.
Still …
I miss the kisses,
holding hands,
making plans.
While the shadows become clear
and the fog lifts
I realize what I yearn for most
are those precious
missing moments …

February 28, 2014

Allen Smuckler

Train Wreck

Do you taste
    divine intervention?
Can you smell
    the painful,
wretched embalment?
Will you recognize the
    art of the
        requiem?

Or
simply
stand-by like a train wreck …

Does time
    heal all wounds
        as they say?
Is age
    just a meaningless
        concept?
Should I
    find a way
to contribute?

Or
simply
stand-by like a train wreck.

Would it matter
    at all in
        the least?
Could the swagger
    of bodies
        retreat?
Should I beckon
    your love
        one last time?
Or
simply
stand-by like a train wreck …

September 27, 2014

sumthin)g wr(g)on

sumthin
)g is wron
g) w/this ma)n
we k(no)w
sumthin
)g is wron)g
4 sirtin

hetrips&falls
& b-r-e-a-k-s
3ribs
sumthin
)g is not
qwite ri)g (ht)
my fr (ien) d

sumthin
g) in/deed is
a   k   w   d
s   e   e
on this

over-easy eg(g
of a day

s….t…..r…….e…….t……chin….
)g a calf
& ten
don
in half…
sumthin
)g is def-i
nite-ly
wr (g) on

Let's :) (: it
mi fri ends
if there'(s) nothin
)g wr(g)on w/
thiz man…Y on
ear(th) does he rite
like th (is)… ;)

January 6, 2015

Allen Smuckler

Fear
(a haibun)

"Dad, feel like having a catch?" I asked quietly. It probably sounded more like a plea, because his response was terse yet melancholy.

"Not right now," he spoke, and for the first time I noticed a tear drop under his right eye.

"Here, come lie down with me Allen," as he tapped the bed gently to show where he wanted me.

I was nervous and confused, but not scared.

"Sure," I said in an agreeable tone.

We lay there, for what seemed like hours until he spoke these words:

"Son, if anything should happen to me, I want you to have my Tallis and Tefillin ..."

I stopped listening after he uttered, "if anything should happen to me"... and went a little numb and cold.

"What could happen to you?" I naively asked, the way any ten-year old might wonder.

What could possibly happen, I thought. All I knew, my father, an orthodox Jew, was bequeathing his most valued possessions to me. His Tallis and Tefillin. Handed down from his father to him and probably from his grandfather to his father.

My head began to spin, my stomach knotted and a sense of panic came over me like I had never felt before.

I was now officially scared, and we both knew it.

side by side
in the stillness of our breath;
we lay

February 21, 2015

Lost

I've dreamt many dreams
remembering only you.
My mind asunder
as time waned,
an indifferent soul,

guided through the rains,
as our yesterdays
continued to disappear.

Lost in a wish
between the tantalizing
unforgettable tunes,
and the unbelievable
turmoil of disbelief,

I was discovered as a child,
scorned as a teen,
replenished as a man,

but lost in the metaphor
of autumn leaves.

May 10, 2015

Heaven's Sake

I sent you away through the desert
when all you wanted was my love
you placed my head upon your breast
and heaven noticed from above

I never thought about the sorrow
nestled in the faraway field
all that mattered was tomorrow
but the scene ended selfishly

I knew what I did was perplexing
my dreams remained under the sheets
my inactions must have been vexing
you waited while I dragged my feet

An orchid remained in the closet
the golden rings left unworn
our meaning was based on a posit
on bibles that never were sworn

I sent you away without warning
when all I needed was your love
rays entered from sun's dawning
while heaven lamented from above.

July 29, 2015

Changing Hats

I changed my hat the other day
became someone I never
thought I would … but I did
I metamorphosed
all because of that hat
it changed me forever
a change in life

I wear many hats you see
of father, husband,
brother and son
cousin, friend and
retiree
but I changed my hats today
to include
an exited lover
and I'll never
quite be the same
I lost a special hat today
which vanished in the mist
it sheltered me from
the storm of life
curled around the edges
it helped me navigate the seas
of discontent and
wonderment

I changed my hat for good I think
It meant so much to me
I couldn't toss it out
so I hung it with the others,
glance at it most every day
and pine away the moments
all because of changing hats
that meant so much to me.

February 9, 2016

DESPAIR

What we call our despair is often only the painful eagerness of unfed hope.

- Mary Ann Evans
pen name - George Eliot
Middlemarch
English novelist, journalist
(11/22/1819 – 12/22/1880)

Burning with Confidence

The fading candle waves on
in our empty Brolio bottle. Living
through its final moments, the
flame gets brighter and
BIGGER
better, more vibrant.
Though only minutes remain,
the flame continues to grow
is more brilliant
than it has ever been before.
It fights desperately to stay alive,
to breathe and remain beautiful
and important.
Anything worth living
must fight until it can no longer
exist.
And then my beautiful, tired candle gets
smaller and smaller
still smaller
until it dies… dies …
dies…
Dead.

May 19, 1968

Allen Smuckler

Ode to Ryan White
(a soulful song)

The disease arched its back,
cradled and crawled
inside the boy's shell

It wasn't his fault,
stricken from birth
he bled all the time

Doctors tried to heal,
comfort with meds.
Transfusions were the method
(of the day)

The insidiousness waited
at the cornerstone of life,
so young, fragile, unfair

Fatefully in need of
blood one day
Ryan only steps away,

began to do and say in vain,
Mama, it's too late to save.

The tainted blood transfused.

His sera mixed with strangers,
backwashed and flushed

frantically…

The innocence left us
alone that day,
and united as one,
we sang a mournful tune.

April 12, 1990

Diary Dreams

DEATH NELL!

NEVER GOT WELL!

WHAT A SMELL!

WENT TO HELL!

oh well…

April 4, 2000

Allen Smuckler

Bitching and Moaning
(Not Seeing the Light)

Buttercups running aloof
in mi cluttered mind
of discontent

Leaflets flapping
as the world turns
mournfully
on its side

Turnstiles of my life
flipping through
the pages of time

yet all i can see
is misery

Flowers cresting
in the space they're
allowed
hoping for the light
the rain...
the time

Memories wafting
by the impulse of wind
billowing, bellowing
the new season
begins

but all i can see is the
scenery of despair

Tormented tides
slapping upside mi head
drowning mi tears
as if i were dead
Wandering dreams
of days future past
i'm trying mi damndest
to make mi life
l...a...s..t.,.

still, all i can see
is languishing fear
bitching and moaning
not seeing the light…

December 1, 2000

45

i've lost the will

i've lost the will
how is it possible
the life of the party
my heart is still
i'm so distressed
what have i missed
the laughter and gaity
i'm such a mess
i sit and ponder
can't help but wonder
my life's adrift
i'm lost at sea

get up i scream
invent a dream
be still my heart
my will be done

for all i've lost
at such a cost
i'm such a you
and you a me
what can I be
when will I see
what have I done
so all alone
in thoughts and fears
i drown in tears
can't help myself

i ask for help
get up you fool
live by the rule
be still my head
my will instead

tortured mind
is so unkind
i've lost the will
there's nothing left
my heart's in ruins
tattered and torn
like a rose bush
with its spiny thorn
i'm collapsed
on the floor
don't know
what's in store
get up i say
find a better way
enjoy the day
my will make hay

i've lost my will
bewildered still
?
I've lost my will
how is it possible
?

August 10, 2011

Allen Smuckler

Mourner's Kaddish
(a prayer for the dead)

יִתְגַּדַּל וְיִתְקַדַּשׁ שְׁמֵהּ רַבָּא. בְּעָלְמָא דִּי בְרָא כִרְעוּתֵהּ,
וְיַמְלִיךְ מַלְכוּתֵהּ בְּחַיֵּיכוֹן וּבְיוֹמֵיכוֹן וּבְחַיֵּי דְכָל בֵּית
יִשְׂרָאֵל, בַּעֲגָלָא וּבִזְמַן קָרִיב, וְאִמְרוּ: אָמֵן.

יְהֵא שְׁמֵהּ רַבָּא מְבָרַךְ לְעָלַם וּלְעָלְמֵי עָלְמַיָּא.

יִתְבָּרַךְ וְיִשְׁתַּבַּח וְיִתְפָּאַר וְיִתְרוֹמַם וְיִתְנַשֵּׂא וְיִתְהַדָּר
וְיִתְעַלֶּה וְיִתְהַלָּל שְׁמֵהּ דְּקֻדְשָׁא בְּרִיךְ הוּא, לְעֵלָּא מִן כָּל
בִּרְכָתָא וְשִׁירָתָא תֻּשְׁבְּחָתָא וְנֶחֱמָתָא, דַּאֲמִירָן בְּעָלְמָא,
וְאִמְרוּ: אָמֵן.

יְהֵא שְׁלָמָא רַבָּא מִן שְׁמַיָּא, וְחַיִּים עָלֵינוּ וְעַל כָּל יִשְׂרָאֵל,
וְאִמְרוּ: אָמֵן.

עֹשֶׂה שָׁלוֹם בִּמְרוֹמָיו, הוּא יַעֲשֶׂה שָׁלוֹם עָלֵינוּ וְעַל כָּל
יִשְׂרָאֵל, וְאִמְרוּ: אָמֵן.

I'm alone I'm alone (as before)
yes alone, yet alone, so alone
I'm alone, I'm alone, shut the door
put the gun to my head, I'm alone…

Yit-gadal v'yit-kadass shmay raba
b'alma dee-vra che-ru-tay,
ve'yam-lich mal-chutay b'chai-yay-chon
uv'yo-may-chon uv-cha-yay d'chol beit yisrael

Magnified, sanctified, God's great name
in the world which He created to his will
He established His kingdom in our lifetime
and during the lifetime of Israel.

My heart is dead, so I mourn for my soul
in this dubious world left alone
screaming wounds from the bottomless pit
Are we left on this earth to atone?

ba-agala u'vitze-man ka-riv,   swiftly and soon
ve'imru amein.   let us say, Amen
Y'hay sh'may raba me'varach   May G-d's great name
le-alam uleh-almay alma-ya.   be blessed for ever and ever.

Bequeath my joy, beneath the voice
I've walked and chosen at the fork in the road
decided which way and lived with the choice
while my mind was about to explode.

Yit-barach v'yish-tabach, v'yit-pa-ar
v'yit-romam v'yit-nasay, v'yit-hadar
v'yit-aleh v'yit-halal sh'may d'koo-d'shah
b'rich hoo. layla meen lol beer-chata,

Blessed, glorified, honored and extolled,
adored and acclaimed be the name
of the Holy One, though God is beyond all
praises and songs of adoration.

Though alone, still alone, is my theme
not quite sure why I feel so alone
I shiver and fear the regime,
in the desert of waterless time.

Allen Smuckler

v'she-rata,   praise and
toosh-b'chata v'nay-ch'mata,   consolation that are
da-a meran b'alma,   uttered in the world
ve'imru amein.   now respond amen

Glory be
and save my soul
Can't you see my dear Lord
I'm alone every day.

Y'hay sh'lama raba meen sh'maya v'cha-yim
aleynu v'al kol Yisrael, ve'imru amein.
O'seh shalom beem-romav, hoo ya'ah-seh shalom
aleynu v'al kol Yisrael, ve'imru amein.

May there be abundant peace from Heaven, and life
upon us and upon all Israel, let us say amen.
He who makes peace in His Heights, may he make peace,
upon us and upon all Israel. Let us say, amen.

Death be not proud on the edge of the bed
and promenade alongside, with my dread.
Father! I hardly knew thee,
Mother and Sister -
too young to flee …

April 26, 2013

49

HOPE

If it were not for hopes, the heart would break.

- Thomas Fuller
British Clergyman and author
(1608 – 1661)

Oscar Scherer State Park
Sarasota, Florida

Perplexity #4

(or Happiness # 1)

Whenever I feel perplexed
about my everyday
Existence,

I simply sit down
with pencil and pad

and wastefully write about
things that are sad.
:
:
:
:

Not this time though.
This is a happy poem.

☺   ☺   ☺   ☺   ☺

January 28, 1972

plasty is nasty

thumping, pumping the ache and pain
was never right had nothing to gain

prowling, growling robbed of all strength
something amiss within arm's length

knowing, growing learn from mistakes
trod with great effort all that it takes

finding, blinding white heat in my chest
look for some refuge a place to rest

frightening, heightening, fears abound
await the cold needle and caustic sound

swishing, wishing all I could stand
never felt much while in la-la land

ballooning, tuning as probe trisects
the team finds a way and resurrects

plasty is nasty I'm sure you'll agree
but dawn's early light is all I can see…

May 7, 2013

Allen Smuckler

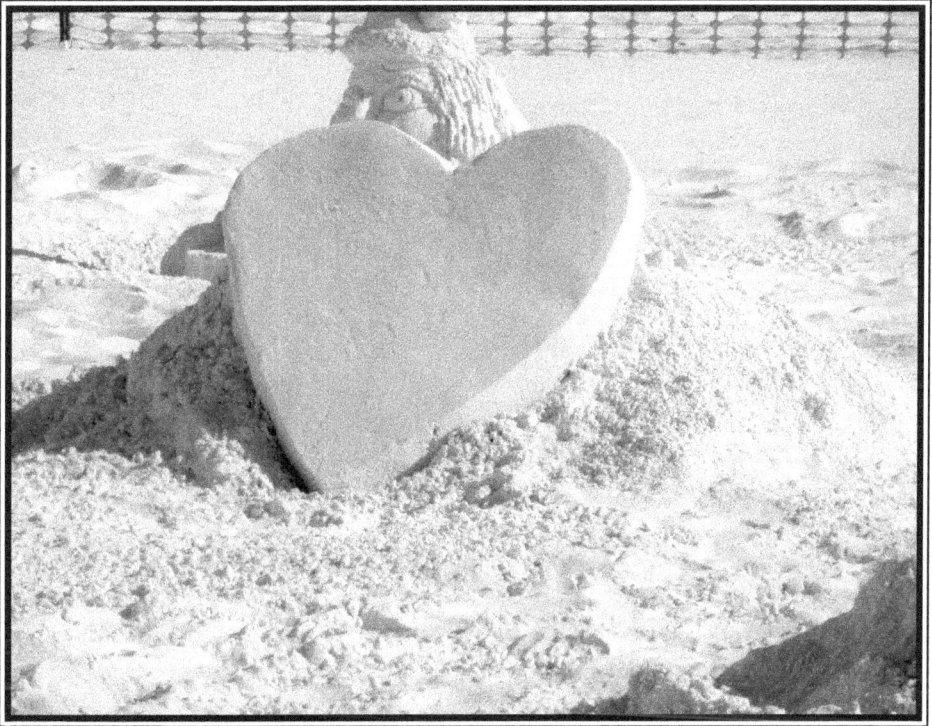

Crystal Classic Sand Sculpturing
Siesta Key Beach
Sarasota, Florida

Change

You have to change.
You have to change
who you are.
You have to change.
You have to change
and be smart.
What matters in life
is more about heart.
You have to change,
be alert to your deeds
and smart to your heart.

Stop telling yourself
you are who you aren't.
You have to change,
be honest at last.
There's nothing to gain
by being alone.
Be true to yourself,
begin from the start.
You have to change,
you have to change,
you have to change
who you are,

so once and for all
answer the call,
be smart to your heart,
understand who you are…

October 10, 2013

Who Me?

me: "I thought you knew."

you: "Knew what?"

me: "What you said.
I thought you knew."

you: "I didn't know.
How could I?"

me: "Could you what?"

you: "Know ..."

me: "Damn!
Are we on the same page?"

you: "Depends."

me: "On what?"

you: "What book you're reading ...
or writing."

me: "Why?"

you: "Why what?
You're making me crazy."

me: "Why?"

you: "Because, that's why.
Jesus, you're maddening!"

me: "Who?"

you: "You! You're freaking nuts."

me: "Yeah, about you."

you: "Who?"

me: "Me…"

November 6, 2014

Our Poem

Courage …
is a tiny word,
but when it's found,
HUGE things take place
in one's life.

I pray before all my days
become yesterdays,
I will find my courage.

Maybe someday,
I will write a poem
that splashes happiness
and joy all over me
full of realizing, instead of wishing
my soul fulfilled, instead of remiss
my mind at peace, instead of amiss

my heart where it belongs,

so I will not be lost
ever again,
and find the courage
to do what's right.

May 10, 2015

Allen Smuckler

Luck
(a haiku)

Leaving Nellie Green's
showers transverse the river –
a rainbow is born

**Branford River at
Nellie Green Restaurant
Branford, Connecticut**

August 12, 2015

A Walk in my Shoes
(a villanelle)

Tidal storms release the spirited pain,
To drink in whatever there is to know;
Take a walk in my shoes through sun and rain.

I ascertain there is nothing to gain,
Mountains erupt and the rivers flow;
Tidal storms release the spirited pain.

The planets circle again and again,
The clouds cover the blue, how apropos;
Take a walk in my shoes through sun and rain.

The Western forest seen by the insane,
Abstain from disdain, like the Carrion Crow;
Tidal storms release the spirited pain.

The feign of self-pity, I must refrain,
Although I know that I would never go;
Take a walk in my shoes through sun and rain.

And you, defined by what is in your brain,
Like a fine Bordeaux, finally aglow;
Tidal storms release the spirited pain,
Take a walk in my shoes through sun and rain.

September 9, 2015

Now

I walked the beach today.
Nothing else to do.
I thought about things
in the rear view mirror,
instead of watching
the road ahead.

I strolled along the shore
by my melancholy self,
let the ripples cross my feet
(adrift) in thought
of what might have been –

I missed another day.

There's nothing in the past
I can do a thing about,
and living in the future
makes little sense at all.
Right now is all that matters,
so, live life while it happens –

and never question why.

February 9, 2016

LOVE

Love is composed of a single soul inhabiting two bodies.

- Aristotle
Greek Philosopher
(384 B.C. – 322 B.C.)

loves, long lost

when love, like a rocket
    (explodes in my pocket)
        & eternity's final tryst
        in the early mist of
        dawn's magical twist
i think only one thought
& feel the beat of
            only
              one
                heart

when peace echoes
    (from my head to my toes)
        in the twilight of my years
        wings of the flawless dove
        scatter my endless tears
i picture only one face
& again i surmise
            only
             through
              haste

the memories of our meeting
  (reminds me of me fleeing)
        from loves, long lost
         exploding from above
        at such a perilous cost
i only seek one hand
to place upon it
           a
            precious
              band

so when fear engulfs my body
  (or anger leads to wrath)
      i, without pause
      call for sandi to speak
      the words i need

March 13, 1970

Allen Smuckler

Siesta Key
Sarasota, Florida

Truth be Told

I have long arms …
I don't know why
I have long arms
but I do,

and I'm proud.

Everyone should have
what I have …
It would make
hugging each other
so much better …

and last
so much longer …

November 23, 2006

Thanksgiving

Take Me In

Take me in you, now ... I'm dying
take a deep breath and inhale me
I love when you do that
and fondle me the way I love
the way you do
your branch-like fingers
with flowery tips...
fondle me ... and never stop
take me in and set me free
let me into your beauty
and change me for life
take me in
take me in ...
and remember where we've been.

January 20, 2010

Allen Smuckler

for them ... for us

The aura emanates from
the beautiful
children
as they look and
discover the reunionized
world we
created

for them ...
Let us be thankful

... and they see and grow
and develop
into who and what
we expect,
desire
and hope will come
to be

Let us be thankful

for them
and
for us ...

... but the landing is
never precise or as
hard as we
imagine
it will be

adults always worry
as children reassure
and offer comfort

for us ...

Let us be thankful for that

... those precious
imaginative eyes
search the universe
for answers
and questions
we never knew to ask

for them ...

... as the world
becomes more
tolerable, acceptable
and children
teach the adults
what it means
to be honest, pure
and that all is well

Let us be thankful

for them
and for us ...

We begin to
change in
order
to realize the
promises
and treasures of
the next generation

and give thanks for them and for us ...

July 10, 2013
revised for Thanksgiving
November 28, 2013

Fragments of Light

Trees deeply rooted in the family garden.
Feeding off the nutrients of each other
helping to nurture … combine and shine.
The nucleus grows, while receding from sight

Important is the growth and lifeline;
the differences and harmonies we learn.
We stand stalwartly in our own way,
graceful in slumber, gazing through the pane.

All that remains are fragments of light,
filtering through the trees in the forest.
Her lustrous, glorious, amber glow
is what I remember, and all she could show.

The ablest and strongest banyan trees
cover footprints on the trodden paths of life.
We recognize the southern sun-drenched winds,
gently push free the gates of heaven.

She no longer remembers the right course,
or the steps to signify which way to go;
nor understands the directions of tides,
or even how to swallow to survive.

All that remains are fragments of light
filtering through the trees in the forest.
Her illustrious, majestic, radiant glow,
is all I'll remember and all that I know.

July 1, 2014

Allen Smuckler

Ringling Museum
Sarasota, Florida

Love rocks
Ryan and Tia's wedding

Musical Sways

You were, and
are, the music
in my life …

I hope
I will
some day
hear the violins
of your heart,
and the
rhythm sections
of your soul …

Nothing matters
more than harmonizing
and performing
a concerto
with the woman
I love …

Let the band play on
and the music
live forever.

Soul Mates

Forever ... or so I thought
from the very first flight
of hopefulness -
to the whispers
of our journey,
our spirits
our distance ...
uncertainty abounded.

Mischievous,
miraculous moments
dreams dashed ...
Daring, dripping desires.
lost in those
unpredictable and
horrifying nightmares
of doubt.

Looking back,
caught in the black hole
of a relationship
that was destined to fail
I decided and believed
from the whole of my heart.

I wouldn't change a thing ...

but the final outcome.

November 4, 2014

Allen Smuckler

Arrival

The world awaits,
eyes closed, lips pursed,
the universe at his feet
hands reaching for the stars.

Journey from the womb
the warmth and security
of mother's loving heart
and father's waiting arms.

He arrives in sync with
no sign of panic or angst,
just a yelp as he enters
and a sigh of relief.

A tear of success
thirsty from the ride,
Cooper meets Mom
in earth's waiting room.

He's placed on her bosom
while Dad comforts both.
The union begins at once
and the three become family.

No one can imagine
what life has in store.
Can we keep him safe
from danger and fear?

All we can do from this day forth
is shower him from head to toe
with rainbows of happiness,
kindness and love …

May 20, 2015

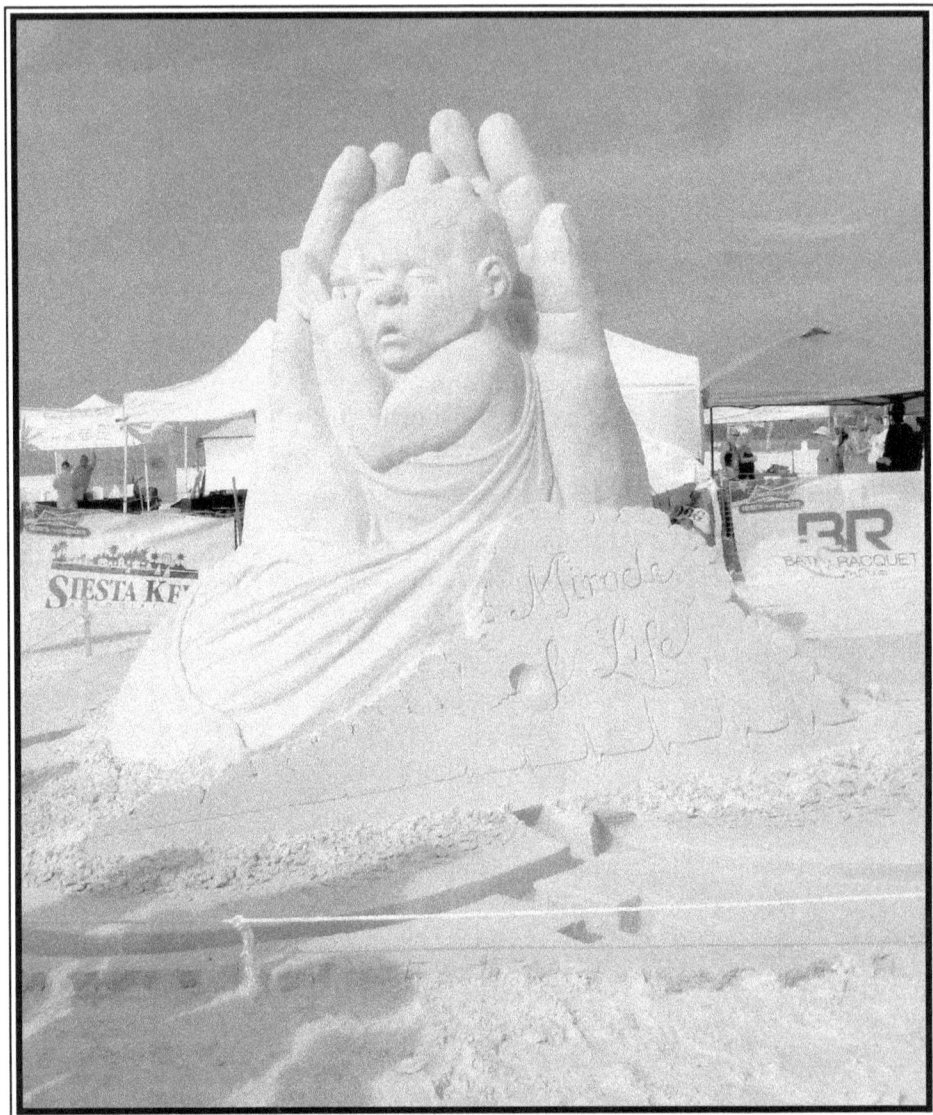

Crystal Classic Sand Sculpturing
Siesta Key Beach
Sarasota, Florida

www.ingramcontent.com/pod-product-compliance
Lightning Source LLC
Chambersburg PA
CBHW031328040426
42443CB00005B/255